OH, REALLY...

(Embracing the "Really" Moments of Life)

By

Tina Ruffin

Oh, Really…

All Scripture quotations are from the King James Version of the Bible, unless otherwise noted.

Copyright © 2019 Contenia Ruffin

All rights reserved.

ISBN: 978-0-578-65137-8

DEDICATION

I dedicate this book to Jesus who is my Abba. This book could not have been written without the breath of the Holy One. God in his infinite wisdom was the mastermind behind the words which hopefully leap from the pages into your heart. I acknowledge him for placing me in an environment that propelled me to grow and go after destiny.

To my children, James, Jordan, and Deanna, for being my inspiration to dig deeper and pull something more out of me so that you could always work to pull the more out of you. I love you more than words could ever express. I am so grateful to be your mom.

To my parents, siblings, and nieces who always show love and support in everything I do, I love you endlessly. I am so grateful that God placed me in a family that exemplifies love with no boundaries.

Acknowledgments

I cannot express enough thanks to all the people (friends, teachers, mentors) who have supported and poured into me along my destiny journey. My sincere thanks go to my Walden Chapel UM Church family for giving me a solid foundation as a child; to Bishop Andrew Fulgham, who has now transitioned to Glory, for planting the seed in me and having the faith that the seed would one day flourish; to Pastor Edward Taylor for watering the seed through your constant words of encouragement; and to Pastor Robert Berry for your mentorship through strong and transparent leadership.

My deepest appreciation to all the fantastic people who have been a part of this project. To my Coffee & Girl Talk family, thank you for inspiring me to stretch myself. You gals rock!

Finally, thank you to every reader who will take something from this book and utilize it to transform your life. You are the reason for me putting pen to paper. If this book helps one person gain a greater understanding of who they are and what they've been called to do, it was well worth it.

Table of Contents

DEDICATION III

ACKNOWLEDGMENTS IV

INTRODUCTION 1

CHAPTER 1 WHAT IS REALLY? 7

CHAPTER 2 I'M CHANGING 11

CHAPTER 3 COMING INTO MY OWN 21

CHAPTER 4 LEVEL UP 30

CHAPTER 5 AWAKE, ARISE, COME FORTH 34

    SELF-AWARENESS: GETTING NAKED 39

    SELF-APPROVAL: EMBRACING YOUR SUPERPOWER 44

    SELF-COMMITMENT: NO EXCUSES 52

    SELF-FULFILLMENT: USE-DA-BEES DON'T MAKE NO HONEY 57

CHAPTER 6 REMOVE THE LUMPS 61

CHAPTER 7 YOUR METAMORPHOSIS 64

CHAPTER 8 BE INTENTIONAL 68

CHAPTER 9 MAKE ROOM FOR WHAT IS NEXT 72

CHAPTER 10 DON'T STOP…GET IT, GET IT! 75

ABOUT THE AUTHOR………………………………………….81

Introduction

I was six months into my new position. It was a typical day, and I had just completed my first big company-wide meeting in Nashville, TN. I was so exhausted and overwhelmed by all the information which had been shared over the last three days. There were all these new expectations, and here I was still trying to grasp the business flow. I was anxious to get home to some normalcy. There's a word – "normalcy" – little did I know my "normal" was about to change forever.

Interstate 240 never looked better. I was glad to be in the car heading in the direction of my house. I didn't call home to announce my arrival because I wanted to surprise my family. The meeting had ended early, and they were probably as eager to see me as I was them. Before my leaving at the start of the week in preparation for the meeting, my husband and I had a huge "heated discussion." That was our code name for an argument. So, we both thought that some time apart would do wonders for us. Well, I had a lot of windshield time to reflect on that "heated discussion" and realized the error of my ways. I was so excited to get to him to say, "I'm sorry." Six hours later, and a stop at Starbuck's, I arrived. *I'm finally here,* I thought. As I drove up, I saw my husband loading things into his car. *He's home early,* was my first thought. *Oh, he must be taking some old stuff to the dumpster.* Upon parking the car, I got out to greet him. "Hi, honey, I'm home. What are you doing?"

The extra-wide smile on my face quickly diminished by three small words he spoke, "I am leaving."

"What?!?!" I'm pretty sure the blood left my face at that moment, while my body became numb. "Where are you going, and when are you returning?" is what I asked.

His response was, "I'm not coming back. You said we needed time apart, and this environment is not working for me anymore."

"Oh, REALLY," was my response. I walked in the house to ensure the kids were okay. And just like kids, they didn't have a clue as to what was going on. They were engulfed in their video games and cartoons.

When they saw me, they immediately stopped what they were doing to greet me and say, "Mommy's home!" *At least somebody is happy to see me,* I thought. So, as the husband continued to move his things, I stood there in disbelief, just watching, and finally, he had the last piece and was gone.

Let him go, I thought. *I'm a strong, black woman. I can take care of myself and my kids. Who needs a man anyway?* – so I thought. All I could think to myself was, *Is this really happening? Is this what open-heart surgery feels like?* was my reaction when I awoke at 5:00 a.m. to the feeling of my heart being ripped from my chest. It was a pain that was indescribable. I did not even feel this when I went through childbirth. *Where's the anesthesia? I need some pain medicine. Can I get an epidural for this?* The tears were flowing uncontrollably, and my breathing was shallow. *What is this, and why is it happening to me?* This was my "really" moment coming to life. I was able to get up from the bed and go into my closet. Once I got inside the closet, a loud wailing noise burst from my soul and out of my mouth. It was the release I needed. The pain I was feeling was the pain of separation. Whenever there is a separation or a cutting away, it does not always feel good. It's like the pain a man feels when he is circumcised.

There is a cutting away of skin that is painful. Marriage gives life, and divorce hurts.

One month had now passed since the husband's untimely departure. I was able to get through the Christmas holiday without crying. This was great for me. The kids and I were preparing for the new year when the phone rang, and it was him, the husband, on the other end. He wanted to know if he could come over so we could talk. As reluctant as I was, something in me wanted to hear what he had to say. So, I said, "Yes…you can stop by." Upon his arrival and greeting the kids, I invited him into the bedroom for privacy.

He began the conversation with, "I need to confess something to you…I've been seeing someone else, and she became pregnant. She delivered the baby yesterday."

"Oh REALLY!" is what I exclaimed! Well, darn, just when I thought this was ending, "really" found me again.

Chapter 1
What Is Really?

Really is a word used to express interest, surprise, or doubt, according to the Oxford English Dictionary. If you break the word down further, you notice the root word being "real." Real has a Latin origin meaning "significant." On that December day, a significant moment had occurred in my life. One that I would forever remember. One that could possibly define my life forever – if I allowed it to.

When these life moments occur, we all think, *There is no way this could be happening to me.* The "really" moments can also be categorized as the moment you connect the dots, or when the puzzle pieces finally line up. You know, after you've been trying for a while to figure something out, and then the light comes on. We sometimes refer to it as the "lightbulb" moment. The moment when light illuminates darkness, a "really" moment occurs. It's a self-actualization moment.

We all have had "really" moments beginning as babies. Think about it…the moment a baby realizes what he or she can do with their legs, like kicking, or using their hands to grab things and hold as they attempt to pull themselves up. Those "really" moments follow us through life, and they expand from there. We go from children to teenagers to adults while experiencing countless "really" moments. These "really" moments become defining moments in our lives, but they are not our final moments. The death of a loved one brings a "really" moment. The loss of a job, the start of a career, a break-up or a divorce, the beginning of a new relationship, marriage, having a baby, etc. are all "really" moments. They are moments we come into our "self." We begin to have a genuine encounter with ourselves. "Really" moments are usually the start of something greater, even though it may not feel like it at the time.

One of my favorite Bible characters to study is Ruth. Ruth had a "really" moment when her husband died, and to top it off, her mother-in-law, Naomi, was now wanting to leave her, too. Ruth was faced with the decision, *Do I leave my country that I have known forever, or do I make the decision to go to an unfamiliar place with my mother-in-law?* So, in her decision to stick with her mother-in-law, it worked out well for Ruth. Not only did she get another husband, but she also got the richest man in the land. Ruth got her Boaz. Remember, a "really" moment may be a defining moment, but it is never your final moment.

Oh, Really…

> *The moment when light illuminates darkness, a "really" moment occurs.*

Chapter 2
I'm Changing

Abraham Maslow, who was a 20th-century psychologist, developed what is known as the "Hierarchy of Needs." Dr. Maslow said that human beings' actions are inspired to accomplish specific needs. These needs are basic physiological needs such as food, shelter, sleep; safety needs such as security, stability, and order; social needs such as love, belonging, and friendship; esteem needs such as being accepted by others and achievement; cognitive needs such as intellectual fulfillment and knowledge; aesthetic needs such as balance and harmony; self-actualization, which is the goal of human development…it is becoming who you already are.[1] The self-actualization occurs when a person can take full advantage of his or her gifts while still being mindful of his or her struggles. The process of self-actualization is different for everyone. Although I had a "really" moment when my husband was packing to leave, and when he said, "I have another child," those were not my self-actualizations moments. They were just moments that began a defining process in me. They were the moments that made me want to dig deeper to see what else had been lying dormant on the inside of me. They were the moments that pushed me to come into my real self – my self-actualization.

People spend years and decades and never encounter self-actualization. People die having never achieved self-actualization in their lives. The graveyard is filled with unused gifts and talents.

---

[1] Abraham Maslow 1908-1970. (n.d.) "A Science Odyssey; People and Discoveries."

Self-actualization starts on the inside and then works its way to the outside, causing an internal change before the external demonstration.

Consequently, people set goals and New Year resolutions and never fulfill them. They desire a new change, but they are not willing to put the work in to get the new change. If you lose twenty pounds, and you still battle with low self-esteem because all your life you've heard people tell you how heavy and overweight you were, you're just twenty pounds lighter, but besides that, nothing else really changed. And what typically happens is that the twenty pounds lost are not maintained. Those pounds, plus additional pounds, show up again. This is because nothing changed on the inside. You got skinnier, but your mind stayed the same. Your thinking stayed the same.

I read an article once where the writer said that most people live through the lens and prisms of others while their true selves remain buried under the levels of other people's expectations. As children, we are conditioned to being what other people want us to be. We grow up doing and being what others say about us. When I began to go through my self-actualization process, I began to ask myself things like: "Why is my favorite color green? Did someone tell me I looked good in green?" As women, mothers, and wives, we tend to take on the form of others a lot quicker than men. We desire to be who they want us to be. Your husband wants a good wife, so you cater to him to ensure that you're just that for him, but all the while, losing your real identity. I realized that the real me had been buried under so many expectations. I never permitted myself to fail.

Men experience an identity crisis as well. They cover theirs with their egos and their pride. I always thought growing up that I wasn't the prettiest, my hair wasn't as long as my sister's hair, my skin was darker than hers, so I used my intellect to propel me. I knew I was smart, so all the while trying to block out the ugly comments, I pretended like I was not affected by those comments. My divorce helped me to see that those comments, along with some others, were still buried. I had still been trying to live up to the expectations of others. So, I would work extra hard to fit in with certain groups of people mainly because this is what I thought I should do. I didn't know "me." I had no clue as to who I really was. Self-actualization sends you on a treasure hunt. There is a treasure in you. "Greater is he that is in you than he that is in the world" (1 John 4:4). It is up to us to discover the treasure.

The great thing about this treasure is that it was put in you the moment you made your arrival into the world. It's always been in you. We fail to sometimes discover it. A treasure hunt requires the proper equipment. People who treasure hunt don't just show up unprepared. They do the planning in advance, and they work to make sure they have the necessary equipment. Your equipment is the word of God. The word of God will help you to discover the treasure in you. The word of God will also help you to eliminate waste and eliminate those expectations that have been keeping you from getting to your place of self-actualization. If this is your first treasure hunt, it's essential to know that you must be appropriately dressed. Attire is another vital component of treasure hunting. Attire must be completed before you begin the actual process of treasure hunting. Before you start reviewing what the word of God says about you, let's make sure that you are correctly dressed. Let's make sure you have been clothed in righteousness through the blood of Jesus. Repeat this with me: *Lord Jesus, come into my life and my heart. I confess that I need to be clothed appropriately. I confess that Jesus died so that I could be clothed in your righteousness. Please forgive me. I need your help with my treasure hunt, so I yield myself to you. I am yours. Have your way in me and through me. Amen!* Wow! That was amazing! You are now on your way to self-actualization. Let the hunting begin!

Here are just a few things the Word says about you:

You are a child of God. (John 1:12)
You are a friend of Jesus. (John 15:15)
You have been justified and redeemed. (Romans 3:24)
You have not been condemned by God. (Romans 8:1)
You are a new creature in Christ. (2 Corinthians 5:17)
You are complete in Christ. (Colossians 2:10)
You are fearfully and wonderfully made. (Psalm 139:14)

The word of God has so much to say about who you are. Take some time to study it on your self-actualization journey. It will be life-changing. Know that while you are starting your treasure hunt, you will have a few things that will try to detour you from completing the treasure hunt. Fear will be your number one deterrent.

Remember you have not been given the spirit of fear but of love, power, and a sound mind (2 Timothy 1:7). Fear has no power or control over you. Those who allow fear to restrict them will never discover the real treasure inside. They will always live a restrictive life. Those who embrace the fear and continue the digging will find that there is more and will embrace the joy of discovering the more. They will recognize that a change is taking place from the inside out, and this change is pretty cool. Susyn Reeve, author of *The Inspired Life: Unleashing Your Mind's Capacity for Joy*, says that there are four aspects to self-actualization:

Being all you can be
Living to your full potential
Honoring and valuing your gifts, talents, and skills, and generously sharing them in service of the highest good for all
Living a life of passion and purpose[2]

---

[2] Contributed by writer Rheyanne Weaver in *EmpowHER*, June 20, 2012

Why settle for mediocrity when there is greater in you? Why settle with living a life of existing when you can live life to the fullest? Why keep your gifts and talents to yourself when there's an entire world in need of them? My dear friend, Tyressa Ty, speaks life into people by encouraging them to follow the *Fiyah*. The *Fiyah* is their purpose and passion. Self-actualization leads you to the *Fiyah*. Find your *Fiyah* today. Don't let another minute, another hour, another day, another month, or another year go by without unlocking your *Fiyah*. The pain and disappointments you've experienced were necessary. The people who left you had to leave you…it was necessary. The job you lost was necessary. The failure was necessary. How else would you have known there was a treasure in you if you never went looking?

Self-actualization starts on the inside and then works its way to the outside, causing an internal change before the external demonstration.

Chapter 3
Coming into My Own

The treasure hunt helped me to come into my own identity. Had there never been a divorce, it may have taken me a little longer to come into my own. Having my own identity has been such a liberating experience for me. It has helped me to know when to say yes and/or no, as well as when to set boundaries and when to let the walls come tumbling down. My life is now filled with "intentionality." Living a life filled with purpose, on purpose, is what I choose to do daily, and it's what I do intentionally daily. My friendships are intentional. My work relationships are intentional. My family time is intentional. My devotion time is intentional. It's so great to feel so free! *Who the Son sets free is free indeed* (John 8:36).

My self-actualization time helped me to embrace the fact that no one else's opinion mattered. What others were saying and thinking about me had held me bound for so long. When I became free from the opinions of others, it was the most breath-taking experience. I mean, I could breathe freely again. It had been years since I was able to do this. Thinking back to the story of Ruth, remember she left the familiar to conquer the unfamiliar with her mother-in-law Naomi. Naomi also had to deal with the unknown. Although she decided to go back to her home country, she would be going back without a husband and children. Moreover, she left full, and now she would have to return empty. Ruth decided that she was purposed to stay with Naomi and see after her. She was determined that she would make Naomi's country her country. Ruth didn't care that she was a

Moabite, and the home country of Naomi was in Bethlehem where all the Jews resided. She didn't care that she probably would get strange looks once arriving in Bethlehem or that when she left Moab, the people would probably ridicule her. None of that mattered to Ruth. She was only concerned with her purpose – which was serving Naomi. As a result of this liberating moment, Ruth received an extraordinary blessing. She found her Boaz and became a part of the lineage of Jesus. I often wonder what would have happened to Ruth had she decided to stay behind in Moab. She probably would have seen a few sprinkled blessings but nothing like she received when she became free from people and walked in her own identity.

Your identity is what you work to create. Frequently, people will allow their past failures, and sometimes successes, define them. I believe that identity is fluid and multi-faceted. I think it's a dangerous thing when you lock yourself into one thing or one way of being. During a time of reflection, I took the opportunity to write down everything I thought others thought of me and all the things I thought about myself. Once I had a visualization of both, I decided that it didn't matter at that moment what others thought; it only mattered what I thought. I was determined not to continue allowing others to dictate my identity. I would take it into my own hands. So, if my thoughts were not lining up with what God thought about me, it was up to me to change that. It was up to me to create the identity that I wanted to live by and grow by. So, I began working to improve every negative thought I had of myself with something that reflected what God said about me. This came through my daily confessions. I would look in the mirror and confess over myself what the word of God said about me. Slowly, but surely, I began seeing myself with a different set of eyes. My talk became bolder, and my walk became more confident. I discovered my purpose, and I began operating in my purpose. I found gifts that had been hidden away in my treasure box, and I began sharing these gifts with others.

When your life lacks true identity, it will take on the identity of those things and the people around you. You will become a ship with no sail and end up in unknown waters. You will take jobs that were never meant for you. Or perhaps get involved in relationships or friendships you were never meant to be a part of. Most people look for identity in both a job and a relationship. A job only adds another layer to who you are, and a relationship only complements the real you. When either of these come to an end, it doesn't mean that your identity has come to an end. It means that another layer of you has been exposed. You will find the real "you" when you expand outside of your comfort zone. My divorce, along with a series of other life events, pushed me outside my comfort zone and forced me to create the list. The list forced me to take a good look at myself in the mirror and work to create the identity that I wanted. It was a stretching moment for me. It forced me into authenticity and out of the fakeness that I had been living for so long. When coaching leaders or facilitating leadership workshops, I often say, "Behaviors drive results…thinking drives behaviors…when you change your thinking, your behaviors change, which produces different results." I learned this from a well-respected leader in our business industry, and it has proven to be a very integral part of my life. I challenge you to change your thinking. You will notice that your behaviors will begin improving, and the results in your life will begin shifting. Now is the time to "Come into your own!" Embrace your "really" moment.

The Hump

Coming into your own does require you to recognize that there is a hump you may have to cross. The hump is like the elephant in the room. You know the elephant is there, but no one wants to verbally say it because this means you must acknowledge that you know it exists. Getting over the hump is not easy, just like getting around the elephant is not easy, but it is necessary. The moment you realize and acknowledge you can't get over the hump alone, the easier it becomes for you. I know, as women, we sometimes think we can do all things. We don't necessarily need the help of others. *I raised these kids by myself. I got my degree by myself. I got the promotion by myself. I make my own money.* And that's all good, but sis, you do need someone else to help. You need someone to take your hand and help you over the hump. Getting over the hump requires you to let go and fully surrender.

Oh, Really…

I knew I had to forgive my husband; otherwise, I would remain in a stuck place. People stay in stuck places for years because of pain and unforgiveness. I realized that I needed to forgive him. My future depended on it. My husband was not a bad man or person. He was just like so many of us who are carried away by our temptations. Embracing my "really" moment revealed to me that forgiveness was the best option, and it had to be done quickly. Why so quickly? I did not want bitterness to enter my heart. Bitterness never comes alone. He is always accompanied by friends, sisters, brothers, cousins, and anyone else who wishes to join the party and take up space in your heart. I had no room for bitterness and all his posse. Bitterness and the crew will take you to some dark places and force you to stay longer than you desire. Get over the hump! You know what your hump is, and it doesn't need to be shared with the world. Just get over it quickly.

Your identity is what you work to create.

Chapter 4
Level Up

Your defining moment can be sometimes compared to the pruning of a plant. Pruning is the process whereby the weeds are plucked up and the dead leaves are removed so that the plant is given the best possible chance to grow and survive. My really moment was a pruning moment for me. It forced me to remove some dead things, get rid of some weeds that had been choking the life out of me, and level up so that I could grow and mature. What's holding you back? What's choking the life out of you? What's hindering you from being the best version of you?

Life weeds happen to everyone at some point in their life span. These are typically things that are unwanted, undesired, and not necessary, which creep into our lives and choke the life out of things that matter to us. Life weeds creep in daily, and they are very elusive in how they get in. For example, the overbooked schedule, Facebook, toxic relationships, debt, Netflix, too many obligations, the job, etc., are all weeds which creep in. We never think that these things are sucking the life out of us. But just like a weed grows alongside a plant and takes up light and water that would typically go to the plant, these things are taking up quality time and space in your life. They're consuming your growth time. And if you want to thrive, you must pluck the weeds. Then there are dead things that we harness for the longest of time. These things are carried around with us, and when wondering why we see no growth, we never stop to remove the dead things. Items such as baggage from a bad relationship/marriage, childhood trauma, toxic emotions, negative thoughts, negative self-image, and the list goes on and on. The truth is that we all have some dead things hanging on that we have grown quite comfortable with. The scary thing about a dead leaf on a plant is that it's not all brown. There may be a portion of the leaf that's still green in color. This is the illusion we have when we think that our lives are fine. We believe we can work around dead things and still see growth. There may be a few green moments, but nothing eternal or consistent. The brown will eventually take over the green, and the plant will become stagnated in its growth until the dead leaf is removed. Your growth will be stagnated until you deal with the dead things. It's time for you to level up. Leveling up means you must deal with your life weeds and get rid of the dead things. You have stood on the sideline long enough watching your life pass you by. Now is your time…today is your day…it's time to level up!

Assess where you are…incorporate all needed resources…celebrate the small victories.

> *What's holding you back? What's choking the life out of you? What's hindering you from being the best version of you?*

Chapter 5
Awake, Arise, Come Forth

You've heard the saying "dead man walking." This is a saying that was adopted from a movie classic in 1995 where the star character, death row inmate Matthew Poncelet (Sean Penn), calls upon Sister Helen Prejean (Susan Sarandon) to help him with one last appeal, maintaining that he is innocent of several murders he allegedly committed. The death row character was trying to do everything in his power to extend his time on Earth. He was not prepared to die, so he became known as the "dead man walking." Death was an inevitable thing for him.

Now isn't this something — he knew that it was only a matter of time before he came face to face with death. Some people walk around every day as "dead men or women." They are dead on the inside. Life has stripped them of living on purpose, with a purpose. They exist. They play it safe when they know deep down, they have been called to do more. There is a hunger and thirst on the inside, but the dead place on the inside of them won't allow them to venture out for more. So, in essence, they become comfortable, fake that they're happy, laugh when all they want to do is cry, and allow contentment to take over, making them very passive. This is their settling place. Mary and Martha reached a settling place when they tried to reach Jesus about their sick brother. In their minds, Jesus's lack of response led to the death of their brother Lazarus (John 11). The two women reached a place where they chose not to believe in the unfailing love of God. They had entertained Jesus at their home. They experienced his glory.

So, it should have been easy for them to take him at his word, but they didn't. They settled with the temporary sight of seeing their brother dead rather than believing in the power of the everlasting king. Likewise, this is an excellent representation of us. We could experience the power of God in our lives, yet we still choose not to believe him on all things concerning our lives. Once we enter the settling place, we pitch a tent, build a fire, roast a few s'mores, and hang out there. And the reality is that it can take years before we transition ourselves from this place. We have allowed past hurt, past failures, and past disappointments to put us in this place where we are now caged in like prisoners waiting for someone to come and rescue us.

Now is the time to cast off your grave clothes and get up. The stones have been removed, and the Greater One is calling you to come forth. The truth of the matter is that we were all spoken into existence for a purpose that is far greater than we could ever imagine or conceive in our small brains. There will always be battles that you must fight. Why? Because two people are living in each of us, who are always at war with each other. Good and evil are in each of us. It depends on the circumstance when one comes out. Put me in the right situation, and the hood, rachet, country version of me might come out. I try to keep a tight leash on her, but now and then she rises just to let others know not to let the smile fool you. Think about Peter. He was Peter, the one who walked with Jesus but also would cuss you out. Then he became Simon, but Peter never left him. It was a battle to keep him suppressed and in check because at any moment he could rise and cut your ear off while cursing you at the same time. Paul was another one. He was Saul, the one who crucified and killed the believers before he ever became known as one of the greatest apostles. But even Paul said, "The thing that I will to do I don't, and that which I will not do is what I keep finding myself doing" (Romans 7:15). You and I are no different. There's a Tina and a Tasha on the inside of me. Tina is the version I work hard to live my life through. But there have been a lot of moments where Tasha would raise her head, and I had to put her back in her place.

> *We have allowed past hurt, past failures, and past disappointments to put us in a settling place, where we are now caged in like prisoners waiting for someone to come and rescue us.*

Ensuring that you allow the real you to awake, arise, and come forth requires a few things in your life: **self-awareness, self-approval, self-commitment, and self-fulfillment.**

Self-Awareness: Getting Naked

How you see yourself has a lot to do with how you live your life. My "really" moment came when I realized that I had not been seeing myself in a clear light, and as a result, I was settling for what everyone else wanted from me. Self-awareness allows you to have a clearer outlook on who you are and what you bring to the table: your strengths, your weaknesses, your opportunities, and even those things that threaten you and prevent you from living your best life.

Studies have proven that when you see yourself clearly, you are more confident, more alert, and more creative. You make better decisions, build stronger relationships, and life possibilities are endless. Self-aware individuals are better leaders, better parents, and better friends. They realize that they don't have to compete with the next person for attention.

Self-awareness comes in two forms – internal and external. The internal deals more with how you see yourself, and the external is how others see you. Being cognitive of your internal self-awareness has a direct correlation with higher job performance, promotions, better social and love relationships, and your overall happiness. Developing in the area of external self-awareness helps you to become more in tune with other people's feelings, and it allows you to show genuine empathy and not be so self-centered. In the business world, we would call this Emotional Intelligence "EQ." Author Travis Bradberry describes Emotional Intelligence as *"the ability to identify and manage one's own emotions as well as being aware of the emotions of others."* There are four core areas of focus with Emotional Intelligence: self-awareness, self-management, social-awareness, and relationship management. Think about it this way: Are you aware of the emotions you generally feel, knowing where they derive from and managing them most efficiently and effectively? After putting your own emotions in check, do you show empathy to others and work to become more enlightened on how they feel and why they feel what they feel? This, in turn, helps us then to focus on the relationship aspect to ensure we are building healthy relationships. The reality is that less than half the population put in the work to fine-tune their EQ. When you look at the top performers in an organization, research shows that 90 percent of them are very skilled in EQ, and they typically make $25,000-$28,000 more than those who are not.

Self-awareness requires a level of vulnerability. It requires you to get naked with yourself. I recently asked a group of women how many of them looked at their naked bodies in the mirror. I was astounded to find out that maybe one in every ten to twenty women look at their naked bodies in the mirror. They typically spend their days doing drive-bys – taking their clothes off, jumping in the shower, running past the mirror until they are clothed. When was the last time you took some time to take inventory of your nakedness? The truth of the matter is that if you can't embrace your physical nakedness, how can you ever deal with the internal issues? You can't get naked on the inside because you haven't learned to deal with the external nakedness. Just because you've been driving a car for years doesn't mean you can isolate when and why the engine breaks down, especially if you haven't been doing routine maintenance. Taking a periodic look under your hood, learning what drives you, and writing it down can become a valuable reference for you.

When you are more self-aware, it becomes a lot easier for you to appreciate others and perceive how they view you in return. Becoming more self-aware puts you on the path to making better choices in your behaviors and beliefs. As you progress in your self-awareness, you will notice that your mental state will change, thereby increasing your EQ. Becoming self-aware is one of the first steps in creating the life you really want. Self-awareness helps you to focus on your dreams, passions, emotions, words, thoughts, and how these things are affecting the life you want. One of the things I use a lot in my personal life, and that I always encourage others who I'm coaching on their career path to do, is create a personal SWOT analysis. SWOT stands for *strengths, weaknesses, opportunities, and threats.* You need to know and see it on paper where your blind spots could be and begin making the necessary changes. Moreover, you also need to know the areas that you're strong in and weak in as well. The SWOT will give you a fresh perspective on who you are. The goal is to become more aware of who you are so that you can drive your life in the direction you want it to go. You're in the driver's seat…now take the wheel.

Here's a brief example of my personal SWOT:

Strength *– Passion/Drive*

Weakness *– Consistency/Routine*

Opportunity *– More attention to details*

Threat *– The daily life demands that may prohibit time for self*

Strengths	Weaknesses
Opportunities	Threats

Self-Approval: Embracing Your Superpower

Are you someone who is always looking for the approval of others? Most of us would probably say "No," but the reality is that we all, at some point in time, have sought the approval of someone else – whether it was a parent, a teacher, a coach, a sibling, a friend, a lover/spouse, a co-worker, etc. That approval typically goes a little something like this: *"How does this look?" "Do you think I should wear this?" "Do you think I'm fat?" "How does my butt look in these jeans?" "Do you think the new boss likes me?"* and the list could go on and on.

Here's a moment for you to get "naked" – not literally, I mean figuratively. This is a "really" moment for you.

Be honest and answer the following questions:

Do you fully accept yourself?	**Yes/No**
Do you like the way you live your life?	**Yes/No**
Do you approve of who you are today?	**Yes/No**
Do you approve of how you conduct your relationships?	**Yes/No**
Do you seek outside approval to make you feel good?	**Yes/No**
Do you judge yourself?	**Yes/No**

Your answers to these questions give you a brief outlook on your approval rating. Is the bulk of your approval coming from you or someone else? Most people are looking for the approval of others, especially the ones we respect and whose opinions we think highly of. You would not believe how many people spend an overwhelming amount of their time compulsively catering to others, doing things against their better judgment, endangering the well-being of family, friends, and ultimately, self to gain someone's approval. This behavior can lead to some very destructive moments in our lives. Moments we must stand back and say, "Oh, really." For example, I spent years seeking the approval of others. I always found myself trying to live up to their expectations of me. Please recognize that this does not happen overnight. These behaviors have been engrained in us for years, and breaking free of them will require some time and process. Disabling this behavior will necessitate that you be diligent, that you persevere, and remind yourself of a few things:

"I am worthy whether or not I have the approval of someone else."

"I am a person who has the free will to choose for myself, and I don't need the approval of someone else."

When we allow other people's acceptance or lack of acceptance to influence how we make decisions in our lives, we are losing our perspective of self-awareness. We lose sight of what's important to us, what motivates us, and what makes us happy. People work jobs for twenty years that they hate and operate in behaviors that they know are counterproductive. They stay in relationships and friendships that they know are dead, all for the sake of companionship and approval. You were not created to go to work, get a paycheck, retire, receive your 401k, and die. You were not created to allow someone to walk all over you, calling you ugly names, and speaking all manner of evil against you. You were created for more. There is more in you. It is time to shift your focus and find your superpower, so you can start today embracing it.

Do you value you? What you value, you will treat differently. I once dated a guy who valued his shoes so much that every time he got home he would immediately take them off, wipe them clean, put them in a shoe cover, and then put them in the box. One day, I took the time to inquire about what the purpose was in doing all that. His response was, "I value my shoes. I spend a lot of money on my shoes, so I want to make sure they stay looking nice." It got me to thinking that he valued his shoes way more than he valued me. It was evident in how well he treated the shoes and how he would blow off things that were important to me. It was another "Oh, really" moment for me. I would encourage you to go back and review your strengths from the SWOT analysis. You can always find your superpower in the strengths you bring to the table. My superpower is passion. I bring passion to everything I do. I would never have come to know this about myself had I not had a "really" moment. That moment shifted the course of my life for the better. Hallelujah!!!

If money was no option for you, what are five things you would do? Take some time to think about this question. This question is a critical step in helping you to become aware of your superpower and stepping out into your destiny without the approval of someone else. A few more tips for marinating on include:

Self-approval comes from the inside. It's your perception of you. It's you, permitting yourself to go after your dreams and your heart's desires.

Self-approval requires that you see the positives in your life. Take time to write down things you are grateful for. I've read that some people keep a gratitude journal. This way they can go back and reflect on things that they are grateful for.

Self-approval requires you to kill the thought of perfectionism. You will never be perfect, at least while you live down here on this Earth. We all have flaws and issues. The key is to know this and still love yourself.

Self-approval necessitates that you stop comparing yourself to others. Subconsciously, we all do it or have done it. *I wonder what it would be like if I were more like her/him; if I were thinner; if my hair were longer; if I had beauty; if I were taller; if I were smarter;* etc. You are precisely the way you were created to be. Your designer designed you the way he wanted you to be. He got so much enjoyment out of designing you. Why would you let him down by worrying about what somebody else thinks of you?

Self-approval allows you to make mistakes. We fall, but we don't stay down. Get back up! Get in there! You were created to win!

Self-approval cancels out all negative talk. Get the trash out of your head and your ears. Are you a garbage disposal or a refrigerator? Garbage disposals receive trash. Refrigerators preserve things. Stuff is placed in both. Which one are you?

Self-approval requires that you spend time with yourself getting to know yourself. Treat yourself to a movie, get a cup of coffee by yourself, take yourself on a trip. You deserve it!

At its core, self-approval is all about loving yourself. Don't wait for others to love and appreciate you. Begin now loving yourself and appreciating yourself. You bring a lot to the table. So what? They don't notice. Maybe they're blinded by their issues. Move on and stop wasting your time on people and issues that require you to step outside of who you are. I realized a long time ago that everyone can't go to the top with me. The higher you go, the tighter your circle must become. And sometimes, you must go by yourself.

Self-Commitment: No Excuses

Now that we've had a few naked moments, and we've shed some tears, let's gear up and get committed. No more excuses! This is what you must tell yourself every day because the old you will occasionally appear on the scene. So, you must be prepared to check her/him at the door. It's time to operate in self-commitment. If you're not committed to you, who else will be committed to you?

Self-commitment requires you to make a promise or pledge to yourself that, come hell or high water, you will not give up, cave in, or quit. *I will run my race with patience, endurance, and long-suffering. I will be all that I've been called to be. Every gift and talent that my creator placed in me will be utilized to its full potential.*

Men and women get married and commit themselves and their love for each other. But what about the commitment to self, before the marriage? When we are first committed to God and then self, we enter the marriage with a different perspective. It's not that I'm vowing to be committed to you because of you. I'm making this vow because of my commitments before your entering my life.

Self-commitment is you declaring that you will do tomorrow what you pledge yourself to today. The key here is to plan. People don't plan, especially for the future. Over sixty percent of people don't have life insurance because they view the future as abstract. They put off today what's needed for tomorrow's successes.

We all have dreams and desires that center around good health and great wealth. But for these to come into existence, there must be a level of commitment on our behalf. We must do the things necessary to accomplish good health, great wealth, and inner peace. Self-commitment needs self-discipline. If you lack discipline, your commitment will quickly move from the top of your list to the bottom. I have tried so many times to lose weight and never could get to where I was trying to be. I finally realized that I had commitment but no discipline. I still ate what I wanted to, worked out when I felt like it, but got on the scale regularly to be constantly disappointed with my weight. *What am I not doing?* is what I asked myself. So finally, "self" answered me back and said, *You're not disciplined. You barely go to the gym, you drink a sweet tea nearly every day, and you're eating ice cream bars at night. You start with good intentions, but those good intentions quickly get lost or left along the wayside.* Without discipline, there is no real commitment.

Those who have been the most successful in their lives and careers were committed to their dreams and aspirations, but they also acted with a level of discipline in their lives. Beyoncé wasn't out partying with the girls every night. She knew that to make great music, she had to be committed to the studio. I recently watched her Coachella performance and her sharing of how she put a plan in place and remained committed to it, even after she had just had two babies. She was disciplined in her eating regimen, her dance choreography, her studio time, and everything else that came with making Coachella a memorable event.

So, why is it difficult for us to remain committed, especially to ourselves? No planning equals no discipline. A plan is your blueprint for the future. An architect never goes to build a house without the blueprints. The blueprint provides a sense of direction on how the house should be constructed, and it helps the architect to remain disciplined and committed to the building of the house. What's your life blueprint? Do you know where you desire your life to be this time next year? In five years? Ten years? Don't feel bad, most people don't take the time to plan their life. The plan gives you something to look at and use to stay the course. Whenever you think about giving up, you can always go back and pull out the blueprint to see where you are and how you get back on track. This is you embracing your "really" moment.

Here are a few helpful tips:

Wake up early and plan your day. Your day should never have control of you.

Meditate or pray. Meditation and prayer put you in a place of hearing. You need to hear clearly, so you can plan a strategy to help get you where you're trying to go.

Embrace change. Change is inevitable. Embrace it quickly.

Don't compromise. Don't compromise your authenticity for someone or something else.

Endure hardship like a good soldier. There will be some hard moments, but you are a warrior. Don't stop fighting and pressing.

Stay the course. Don't let other people take you off track with their motives and agendas.

Get rid of the toxins. Toxins are the people, friendships, relationships, bad habits, etc. that you have acquired, and they are now depleting you of life and energy.

Live every day. Live every day like it's your last day. Be happy. Celebrate the small victories. Laugh. There is no easy way to success. Success requires hard work, commitment, and discipline. You must be dedicated to being a better version of yourself. Choose wisely what you commit to. It's your level of commitment that will drive your level of success.

Self-Fulfillment: Use-da-Bees Don't Make No Honey

I once heard one of the most fabulous motivational speakers, Les Brown, say this: "Use-da-bees don't make no honey!" It took me some time before I truly understood what he meant by

Oh, Really...

that. Once I grasped it, I took hold, and it has always been with me. Mr. Brown had a unique way of making the simplest points. This saying alluded to the fact that if people know you as a "used to be," you probably have stopped living and dreaming.

Self-fulfillment is the act of one fulfilling his or her hopes and dreams. Mr. Brown pointed out to millions of people that just because you fulfill those hopes and dreams does not mean you stop dreaming. There should be a moment of celebration and reflection, and then back to work. We should never think we've arrived, or we're done. Life is about growing and stretching. If people know you as a "used to be," what mark are you making? It's not about what you used to do. Circuit City and K-marts are known as "used to bes." They used to be in business, but now they're not. Busyness is not self-fulfillment or even success. Just because someone looks busy, doesn't necessarily mean they are accomplishing anything. Those living unfilled lives usually cover it with working harder and longer to make more money so that others don't see the missing pieces. Self-fulfillment comes from the inner you – your knowing what it is in life you truly want and not allowing society to put its thoughts and beliefs on you. Self-fulfillment cannot come from material things. The fulfillment you're needing is a change of mindset. It's you, shifting your outlook and finding contentment and happiness in something you consider important and not what others want you to do.

Take the time to:
Surround yourself with positive thoughts and positive people.
Visualize what success looks like.
Take charge of your own life.
Celebrate often.

Changing your focus to reflect more on the positives allows you to quickly identify the holes

Oh, Really...

and make the necessary changes to live your best life today. It will not happen overnight. It will take time and lots of effort on your part. You got this. Soar like an eagle!

Chapter 6
Remove the Lumps

I remember watching my aunt make biscuits from scratch. One tool I recall her using was a sifter. The sifter has a wire net in the middle and a handle on the side which allows you to turn it or shake it. She would pour a cup or two of flour into the sifter and begin to turn the handle. So, I asked, "Auntie, what's the handle for?" She responded and said, "It helps you to get out the lumps." Now thinking about how fine flour is to start with, *How could there ever be lumps?* I remember thinking.

The lumps can develop from the flour sitting on the shelf. The flour becomes packed down, and the sifter helps to break things up more evenly. Sifting not only removes the lumps, but it exposes the flour by pushing it through the fine holes in the sifter. Once the flour is sifted, it is much lighter and easier to use which makes mixing the other ingredients with it simpler.

Contentment and complacency can cause lumps to develop in your life. Even after going through a period of self-approval and self-commitment, there will still be things that must be sifted from your life continually. These things will work to creep back into your thought life. If they can find a way into your head, they can eventually find a way to your heart. The lumps come in all forms, sizes, and shapes. Just when you think that things are settling down in your life, here comes a lump. A regular sifting will help eradicate the lumps. Some recipes call for sifting the flour, while others don't. However, any good baker will tell you it is always in your best interest to sift the flour.

Sifting for us is our way of reminding ourselves, consistently, who we are. It takes us back to a place of self-awareness. The sifting helps to ensure we keep our thought life together. Your life will typically move in the direction of your most influential thoughts. Changing your outlook of how you see yourself is a daily battle. Use your sifter regularly.

> *Your life typically moves in the direction of your most influential thoughts.*

Chapter 7
Your Metamorphosis

Most people live their lives through the lens of a caterpillar instead of a butterfly. The world through the caterpillar's lens is very small. A caterpillar spends the bulk of its life crawling and only going so far in its life cycle. Although the caterpillar tries to crawl and climb higher, he is only able to see or get so far. He is limited by outside factors. He decides to eat and eat some more hoping that one day he will grow large enough to see what his friend the bumble bee sees. His purpose is unknown and unimaginable. It's not until he goes through metamorphosis that he truly begins to understand that there is something more to him. It is at this stage that he realizes in order to have a future, a transformation must take place.

Year after year, day after day, hour after hour, second after second, we go through life not seeing or even imagining that there is a better version of us. For us, living daily and working to stay afloat where we are is the highlight of our lives. Staying on the level of a caterpillar robs you of ever seeing the next version of yourself. We get to a place of contentment, and it is this contentment that robs us of our future self.

The caterpillar finally gets to a place where he has grown all he can in his current body and state. He then begins to figure out another method of survival by hanging itself upside down from a twig or branch and spinning itself into a cocoon. The cocoon is the hiding place or can be seen as the waiting place. He waits there to see what else will happen. But while he is waiting, he is in a place of isolation, a place of darkness, and a place of being alone. It is also a place of struggle. For the caterpillar to experience the next stage of growth he must shed his old skin, and this can become a struggle. His body struggles to break itself down so that something else stronger and more beautiful can be birthed. To reach your butterfly stage, you will have to shed some things – depression, fear, doubt, people, etc. Anything that is preventing you from getting to the next version of you must go.

Oftentimes in life we place ourselves in a cocoon. When struggles arise, we go to a place of darkness and isolation – a place where we immediately feel we are alone and must endure the struggle on our own. The struggle was never meant to drive us to darkness but to a place of light. The caterpillar's struggle is all a part of his growth in order to become the butterfly. Your struggle is necessary for your growth, but you do not have to go through it alone. You have a savior who is there leading you through the dark places. And all the while he is leading you, he is growing you and strengthening you.

After metamorphosis the caterpillar is able to break out of the cocoon and emerge as a beautiful butterfly with wings. Your metamorphosis is a temporary state. You are filled with purpose, and your purpose is causing you to burst free of the cocoon that has held you bound for so long. There is a butterfly on the inside of you, and it is ready to fly.

> *Year after year, day after day, hour after hour, second after second, we go through life not seeing or even imagining that there is something greater on the inside of us.*

Chapter 8
Be Intentional

Saturday mornings are the absolute best for me when I don't allow my schedule or other people's schedule to dictate how I spend my morning. I normally wake early to get my day going. I'm focused on completing my Saturday chore list around the house and then any necessary errands that must be completed. If the kids have events, they must be factored in along with any other events I've committed myself to earlier in the week. The Saturday morning I long for is one that involves me staying in bed past 7 a.m.; one where I don't hear a knock on my bedroom door and someone on the other side asking what's for breakfast; one where my phone isn't ringing off the hook and someone is asking what time will I arrive and, well, you get the picture. Since it had been such a long time that I experienced what I would deem a free Saturday morning, I decided to make one. Earlier in the week I canceled all Saturday activities. I placed a Do Not Disturb sign on my door the night before. I left a note on the kitchen sink to my kids saying, "Don't call me and I won't call you." I turned my cellphone off, well, not off, but on silent. It was the best feeling ever.

I woke early just like I normally would, but I didn't feel rushed to get out of bed. As a matter of fact, I turned over to see how much more sleep I could get. Finally, when I did wake a few hours later, I got up, completed my daily hygiene regimen, put on some coffee, and took a moment to just sit. I never could have had this moment of what I considered solitude if I hadn't been intentional in my planning.

Oh, Really…

We live our lives on the go, and there is a very small amount of intentionality. Being intentional means being deliberate, being purposeful in word and action, making thoughtful choices, and responding versus reacting. Intentionality forces you to make a plan and not excuses. It brings alignment into your life. It drives you to want to do more than just exist and get by. It pushes you to become more engaged in your life. For this next level of your life, intentionality must become your friend. It must be a member of the friendship circle. You need him. Intentionality will keep you focused on what's important to you.

Intentionality forces you to make a plan and not excuses.

Chapter 9

Make Room for What Is Next

There I was, window shopping at one of my favorite shoe stores, when I had this impulsive reaction to go in and purchase a new pair of shoes. I had just told myself a few weeks prior that I would not be purchasing anything else until I took time to make room in my closet for new items. The problem with this is that it is my belief that I need to retain everything in my current closet, and just work to fit in any new items. There are things which are very dear to my heart in that closet. For example, various items that I once enjoyed wearing but, because of time coupled with a few extra pounds, I can no longer fit any of those items. But why throw them out when I can just keep them for later usage? I know what you're thinking. You're thinking that this would probably add more clutter to the already cluttered closet. Just throw it out and make room for the new.

It is so easy to say, "Get the clutter or junk out of the closet," but what about the clutter and junk in our lives that stop us from experiencing the new? I once had someone tell me that in order to experience something new in your life, you must create the space for it. Creating the space for the new forces you to focus on the old and make the decision to get rid of some things. Making room for what's next will sometimes put you in uncomfortable moments, but it's your embracing of these moments that will allow the new to come in. If you are filled to capacity, you can't expect anything new. Where will it go? At some point you must acknowledge that there are some things and some people who are taking up space for what's next in your life, and they must go. You need to pour out so that you can receive what's next in your life.

> *Creating the space for the new forces you to focus on the old and make the decision to get rid of some things.*

Chapter 10
Don't Stop...Get It, Get It!

I can remember during my early college years, there was a popular song by Uncle Luke and the Two Live Crew called "I Wanna Rock." When this song came on, we would tear the club up. Let's be honest; if the song came on right now, I would tear the floor up. It was one of those songs that made everything in you come alive, and you did not want to stop. You wanted to continue getting it in! So, if Uncle Luke could end his song with an anthem to all dancers to not stop but get it, get it, why is it that we get to a point in life and stop? We stop getting it. We stop living. We stop laughing. We stop loving. We just stop!

Life is not intended for us to stop. Life is given to us to live. You stop when you're six feet under. When the first man and woman were created, they were told to be fruitful and multiply. "Be fruitful" doesn't necessarily mean having a lot of babies. It means living a life of purpose, on purpose, regardless of the "really" moments that may come your way. The greatest tragedy in life is to live with no purpose. A purpose is more than you being a wife, mother, husband, etc. Those are roles you have in your life. We are all created for a purpose, and a purpose is placed in us to fulfill. An apple tree has a purpose, and everything attached to that tree has a purpose. It begins as a tiny seed going into the ground. The seed must endure some things. It has to withstand weather temperatures, whether there is enough rain to water it, or whether it is too hot or cold. The seed endures and produces a tree. The tree then produces fruit. The branches on the tree serve to hold the fruit until it is picked. The leaves provide the oxygen to you and me to live. There is a purpose when the tiny seed goes in the ground. Just like there is a purpose for the apple seed, there is a purpose for us.

You must not stop living. You must go after your best life today. You may lose money, but don't lose time. You can always get your money back. Eight out of every ten millionaires have filed for bankruptcy at least once. Abraham Lincoln's life, in my opinion, is one of the most significant examples of failure and persistence wrapped in one individual. He is a specific example of someone who did not quit but kept getting it. Lincoln was born into poverty and lost his mother when he was very young. He lost eight elections, failed in business at least two times, lost multiple Congress and Senate races, and was institutionalized for a nervous breakdown. President Lincoln could have quit so many times, but he didn't. And because he chose not to quit due to his circumstances, he became one of the greatest presidents in the history of our country.

There is never an ideal time to start pursuing your dreams. You're waiting on the right time. You're waiting to go back to school. You're waiting to start the search for the new job. You're waiting to quit the current job. You're waiting until you get your money right. You're waiting for the kids to grow up. You're waiting until you get married. You're waiting until you get divorced. Well, let me tell you, you're waiting at a bus stop where there is no bus. You keep peeking around the corner to see if the bus is coming, and it's not. There will never be an ideal time, and life will continue to pass you by. Be like Nike and "Just do it!" Do it afraid. Do it with no money. Do it alone. Just do it. A roadmap to help navigate your path requires you to:

Be Driven. Your drive is like gasoline for a car. Without gas, the car can't go anywhere. The drive is what keeps you going. It's your vision. Write it down. Keep yourself in remembrance of it daily.

Be Relentless. Regardless of what comes your way, decide that you will not quit. The palm tree is the most relentless of trees. It keeps getting hammered in the heavy downpours and the fierce winds. Just when it looks like it's going to break, it bounces right back in place. There will be rain, and there will also be mud that comes as a result of the rain. Don't get stuck in the mud.

Now is the time to go after it. Go after all your dreams, aspirations, and heart's desires. Even if you must do it with a limp. Jacob decided to wrestle all night with an angel of the Lord until he received his blessing. He didn't care that the wrestling left him with a limp. It didn't stop him from walking or running. It meant that maybe he couldn't walk or run as fast as the next person, but he could still move.

Don't let the limp stop you. The more you walk, the easier it becomes. Today is the day you embrace your "really" moments and live life to the fullest. Dream bigger. Dance in the rain. Raise your standards. Be all you have been designed to be while embracing your "really" moments of life. Remember, the "really" moments are not final moments, but they are defining moments. Your new life is waiting for you, sis. Go get it!

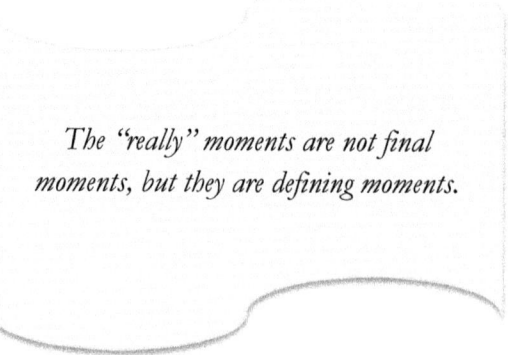

The "really" moments are not final moments, but they are defining moments.

About the Author

Tina Ruffin is a visionary, speaker, coach, trainer, and entrepreneur, who uses her energy, humor, and passion to capture the attention of nation-wide audiences. With over 20 years of experience, she utilizes the T.R.E., a.k.a. Tina Ruffin Experience, to compel individuals to move out of their comfort zone by focusing on key behaviors which stagnate growth and cripple success. She boldly challenges you to explore the inner most parts of your being by sending you on a personal treasure hunt and discovering that the best part of you is still waiting to be lived. Tina specializes in Training and Talent Management. She is a dynamic speaker and trainer, and has exceptional platform facilitation, coaching, and course design skills. She is the CEO/Founder of Coffee & Girl Talk, LLC.

Coffee & Girl Talk is an empowerment move giving life to women of all ages through meaningful conversations centered on biblical principles. It was birthed in a small coffee shop with a group of women who shared like-life experiences.

The group challenges individuals to Move Out of the Comfort Zone and live a life full of abundant living. Life happens in circles. Coffee & Girl Talk places an emphasis on abundant living through social-awareness, self-awareness, and professional development activities.

The participants represent a vast diversity of race, socioeconomics, and cultures. The diversity adds to a circle of life-long friendships, a greater collective impact on the local community, and a strong network of peers and mentors.

Tina serves as Director of Talent & Development at Irby Company – a Sonepar Company located in Jackson, MS, where she fulfills the role of sales/leadership coach, facilitator, curriculum developer, and trainer.

Oh, Really...

For More Information:

Website: www.tinaruffin.com

Email: tinaruffinexp@yahoo.com

Facebook: www.facebook.com/TinaRuffinExp

Instagram: tinaruffinexp

Twitter: @tinaruffinexp

Phone: (662) 590-2966

Milton Keynes UK
Ingram Content Group UK Ltd.
UKHW050749210324
439796UK00015B/1390